What's Hid Beneath the Bones of This Great Tree

What's Hid Beneath the Bones
of This Great Tree

An Epic Journey

for Berta —
in gratitude for this
journey into wilderness
we
share.

Chris Erdman

RESOURCE *Publications* · Eugene, Oregon

WHAT'S HID BENEATH THE BONES OF THIS GREAT TREE
An Epic Journey

Resource Publications
An Imprint of Wipf and Stock Publishers
199 W. 8th Ave., Suite 3
Eugene, OR 97401

www.wipfandstock.com

PAPERBACK ISBN: 978-1-6667-0964-3
HARDCOVER ISBN: 978-1-6667-0965-0
EBOOK ISBN: 978-1-6667-0966-7

JULY 15, 2021

for you who share my love

of trees and all the mysteries

their roots embrace

There is a pain— so utter—

It swallows substance up—

Then covers the Abyss with Trance—

So Memory can step

Around— across— upon it—

As one within a Swoon—

Goes safely— where an open eye—

Would drop Him— Bone by Bone.

—EMILY DICKINSON, Poem 599, 1862

Contents

among our darkened roots there works
a sacred alchemy

part one | *awaken*

a voice speaks —

Somewhere deep inside the Earth, something familiar lives.

I feel it in my bones.

I heard a sigh just now—a gasp that's rising from the Earth beneath my feet, as if some sad and hidden thing tried desperately to let itself be heard. A wisp of memory flits through my brain, then flees and leaves a hint of what it tried to say. I taste the color blue; midnight in its hue and bitter in my mouth. Suddenly I'm cold, and sad, a sorrow deep and unexplained. This sadness is a heavy weight; it pulls me down, my cheek pressed to the ground in grief I neither want nor understand.

The stars have fallen from the sky. The Earth's in disarray. The gods are dead or fled before this travesty.

But something living's hidden deep among the bones of this Great Tree.

the man speaks —

I find myself out on a broad but sterile plain.

I sit astride a horse. We plod along a well-worn path. Though a large and handsome beast, my mount seems dull and follows aimlessly the only path in sight. It seems depressed and out of life.

Since I am only waking up, I'm bound to let the creature stay the course till I make some sense of what I ought to do. Around me, grey and barren hills. Not a single tree or shrub. Nothing dares stand up at all. A stagnant creek runs toward the middle of the plain, draining to a foul lake. Not a single bird to sing or fly.

A boy plays in a field of green—mirage or memory, I cannot tell. A blue balloon excites his energies, as much as any friend could do. Joy quivers through his small, lithe form; wild exuberance painting him as red in face as sky-blue is his toy. An angry shout, a shot rings out, a man with smoldering gun. The balloon lies dead upon the Earth as the man berates his son. The child drops his head, then turns, and walks stiffly toward his lifeless friend. A shudder quavers through his fragile frame; he contains the inner quake. Then tearless and stiff-lipped he falls instead upon the blood-soaked ground, slips silently inside the Earth, and quickly disappears.

I watch it all from far away and find myself unmoved. It seems impossible to feel in this abysmal place.

Still we plod along the wandering way, through landscapes bare and dry. The horse's head droops listlessly, and mine bobs to and fro; I am not fully stuppored, but neither am I full awake.

And yet, I'm free enough from inner fog to note that just ahead the pathway forks; a lesser path leads up a hill, while the greater winds along the plain.

Despite my murky mind I can make out what looks to be a band of living things draped round a great and solitary mound. The sight of trees stirs in me a feeling long asleep. Eagerly, I spur the horse onto the lesser path and toward the mound encircled by the trees.

The trees draw me, curious yet not unafraid. In truth, these verdant creatures repel as well as lure me after dwelling long in that lifeless land. They stand so close, kinfolk in the forest clan. They touch and breathe and feel; they sway and whisper, drink the sky and eat the Earth. So unlike me.

I am afraid—of the living things that lie before me, of the dead I leave behind.

And yet, despite my fright, I spur my mount and pass beneath these living arms into the lush and fearsome darkness of the wood.

the forest speaks —

Wounded, they come to us, man and horse, into our verdant house. Neither one what they once were, what they could be, nor what they will become. We see all that. Trees know far more than men, whose roots aren't merely shallow, but stunted, disconnected from the Earth by their foolish need to run or ride.

Long before they entered us, we felt them come.

Earth, which feels and follows every step upon its crust, hummed the news of their approach. Stones and worms picked up what Terra spoke. They told our roots. Roots told the moss and ferns and creeping things. And word spread up and out until the farthest reaches of our canopy was bustling with the news.

We knew they'd come. They had to come.

The man is not privy to this truth. Not in his head. But something in him knows—the part where knowing's done, deep among the bones of man and Earth and stars. Deep among the bones where gods arise and pull him back into the Earth.

Dark matter. Quantum loam. The humus of the Earth. Here are the gods that cannot die. A god groans deep within our bones. Our forest body vibrates with the sound.

Man and horse stop in their tracks. They look as if they feel it too.

a voice speaks —

Our wounds would want us to forget, and to forget we'd like to lose the key to what is felt. But what's forgot is never lost. It breathes. And sighs. And waits.

the man speaks —

The trees stand close here in the wood. Too close for me; there's hardly space for me to breathe. After my long wandering upon the deadening plain, this living wood oppresses me with life.

Light skinned, spindly birch in ghettoed groves; gnarled alders, wandering free within the wood; they tease the regimental pines who march like soldiers on parade. The air feels dense, thick with the musk of dying things lying heavy on the Earth, the muck that feeds the awfulness of life.

This verdancy, its energy, the murmur of the trees, the story going on beneath: all this makes me more afraid than when I walked or rode upon the sterile fields of my disaffected state.

With each footfall of my horse, my foreboding grows. I am now full-awake, my mind alert, my senses piqued. The wood is loud with life.

Suddenly, the forest parts, we find ourselves within a spacious glade: a vast clearing, carpeted with grass. And planted just within the arboreal ring, stands a ring of stones, the end of each sunk deep into the Earth, each twice my length in height.

A massive mound rises from the center of the ring, and there upon its crown, a tree—a tree so great, so old it's hard to fathom it was ever like the lesser trees that circle round, trees that look as if they worship at its feet.

It seems the Pillar of the World.

a voice speaks —

Some have said that fear is where wisdom finds its start. Not true.
Fear wants to freeze the mind and heart, or make them flee away.
Wiser to say that awe, not fear, is the surest way to truth. Awe
opens up what fear would lock away.

The key to what is locked inside is grief.

part two | *descend*

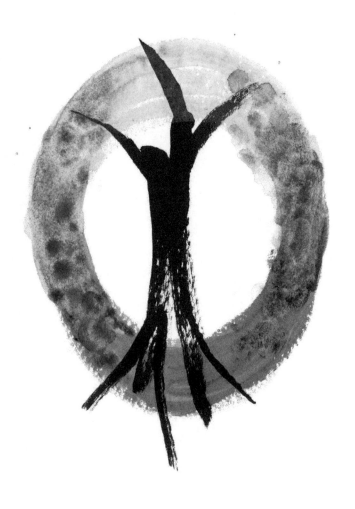

the man speaks —

In near disbelief at this, what some have worshipped as divine, I dismount and give my horse to graze amidst the stones. Then step by step, and round the hallowed mound, I climb like a pious pilgrim toward a shrine. I'd go forward on my knees—a penitent en route to Rome or Compestola—but the gnarled roots of this Great Tree keep me on my feet.

There's a forest in the branches above my head, another in the roots beneath my feet. The canopy above, a world unto itself, held up and nourished by all that is below. And what's below is kin to all that is above.

Two worlds—each cannot be without the other—constellated by the living body of this Tree's colossal trunk.

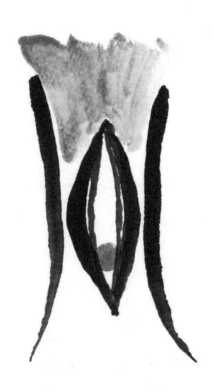

Round the far side of the Tree, I come upon a cleft in its great trunk. The passage to the cave within barely wide enough to fit a single unencumbered man. Drawn by intrigue and perhaps some primal pull, I slip inside.

It's dark and cool within these smooth and fleshy walls. The air is moist and thick. I taste the humid musk, and stray a thought toward that other verdant place—the smaller cleft between a woman's legs.

My eyes adjust and as they shift to see inside this darkened room, I'm made aware that I'm not the first to wander through that door. A shell or pebble here. A feather there. Some old candles, having long ago burned black the wall above and dripped pale beeswax on dark tree-flesh below.

I wonder: was this the journey's end for someone else, or had it just begun?

Each step I take is down, a downward drop into the depths, into the dark.

I'd stumbled through a second door, inadvertently, when in a moment of repose, I leaned against the insides of the Tree, bemused by a fantasy that I might feel it breathe. I'd fallen through the door and caught myself in time to keep from tumbling down an ancient path of steps that clung among descending roots of this inverted canopy.

Down among the roots I climb, my pathway lit by fading light that falls from the narrow doorway far above. How many faltering steps I take, I cannot tell. Time's as still as the ancient and unmoving air I breathe.

Twice I slip and fall and catch myself, dangling from a step hung between two gigantic roots. There are no walls along these steps; they're held in place by the tangled roots from which this stairway's strung like some great beaded necklace hanging there in space.

More times than I can count I think to turn around, but can't—or won't. I'm driven by some inner need or quest that overruns my fear.

a voice speaks —

Our world has too much loved the light. We think there's so much more to see beneath the glowing sun. But night has things too— things day will never see or know. Some want noon, but those who'd grow would have a night without the moon.

the man speaks —

It's pitch black now. I no longer see the hand before my face. I freeze in place. There is no going back, and now, no next step down into the dark of this great deep.

What foolishness has led me to this place? If I don't die first of fright or thirst, paralyzed upon this ledge, then my next step, either up or down, will end my life. I'll surely fall into the vast abyss.

I berate myself for turning from that road far up above, when, astride my horse, I chose to turn away and toward this path into the darkened earth.

Why not have stayed the course, though half dead?

Better that, than what I too soon may be . . . full-dead.

I'm lost inside unending night; I cannot tell how long it's been. I cry for help but the sound of my own voice is swallowed by the gloom. There's no one here, no God of love. I am alone, forgotten by the world above.

One age passes, maybe two. But then a sound comes to my ears. So slight, at first I think it's just a thought inside my head.

It grows, slow but unmistakable. It wanders through the tangle of my fears, floating up from down below and past the voices in my head that blame and rage and contradict. What drifts up and into me sounds something like a church—not new, but old—like monkish choristers engaged in sacred song, the opus of their vigil sung when deep into the night.

A tiny star appears, a mere pinprick of light—not up above as it should be, but far below, as if all nature's tipped itself from head to toe.

I rub my eyes, my mind not trusting what it thinks it sees.

The star remains, as does the song. I press myself beyond my fear and, wild with desperation now, slip down another stair, taking care to feel for that vital contradiction that separates a stony shelf from the thinness of pure air.

So far, so good. And now, determined by a mad desire to meet with other souls in this dread place, I slide myself down one more shelf.

I move too quick; I slip—and then, with gravity a heavy hand pressed down upon my weakened state, I'm thrust out and down and toward the deep. I'm twisting like a tree-rat that's tumbled off a branch; I spin and turn, battered by roots that hang into the night—grasping, frantic for any chance to break my fall and keep me from the gaping maw of death.

As I fall, the song becomes a shriek; the light of that Earth-bound star, once a pinprick against the night, now looms below—a widening glow that speaks to me of hell.

And then, just when I wish I'd died upon the coldness of the stairs above, and not inside the awful fire awaiting me below, my body slams into a giant root. It breaks my fall; I slide, wounded, down an inner arm of this Great Tree, and crumpled, motionless upon a stony floor, I slip, unconscious, into a painful, dreamless sleep.

part three | *arise*

I wake to find myself upon the threshold of some great hall hewn long ago from solid rock. The song has ceased, but now, a golden light flickers from a score of torches keeping watch upon the walls.

My body aches; I thirst. The blood thrums in the temples of my head. I sit, then slowly come to stand and survey the place I'd come to dread.

There's nothing in the hall. No sound at all. At the farthest end, a door, not large, the size of a common entryway. And in the door, a small window barred with steel. Beside the door, a heap of filthy rags—the only other thing, beside myself, in this bare hall.

The door is made of wood and fastened to the stone with iron forged in ages past. The workmanship is hardly fine—it speaks of one who simply meant to hold something inside. These hinges, though resembling those that turn, have not moved in many years.

The window's small, only large enough to vent the space beyond the door. Between the grid of iron bars I peer, and see inside, a mound, and near its top, buried to his neck, what looks to be a child—a boy of ten or twelve—facing toward the back of that grim space. The thick gloom beyond the door makes it hard to make him out—the torchlight of the hall casts scant light between the bars. My head is in the way. And as I stare inside against the gloom, there's barely light enough to see inside the cell at all.

What I make out is this: a boy is being buried, like an ant trapped in some great hourglass. Sand falling down upon his head. He takes it all and neither moves nor cries for help.

I don't even know if he's alive.

I search the door for a latch and find, to my distress, there's none. Just a wooden slab with iron tangs, manacled to stone. I push against the door, shout at the boy within. The door won't budge; nor does the boy. Nothing moves save sand upon his head.

But then—a gasp, a slight groan, as if a frightened thing is wanting to be known.

I move along the wall looking for what might be the key to open up the door. Kicking through the filthy rags I'd seen before, I find a withered man slumped there instead. He's old and thin, nearly dead himself, his eyes gone white with cataracts. Desperate now, I yank him to his feet and pull him close till I can feel his fetid breath upon my face.

"The key, old man! Where's the key to this damned place?"

He smiles a grim and toothless grin then chants, "Foolish man, neither God above nor gods below can open what has once been closed. The key you seek is in the tears bound up for far too many years."

"A riddle and a rhyme? I get a jester at so grave a time? A password, key, or secret route into that cell—and tell it now—before I break your foul neck!"

He laughs at me and shakes his head and mocks my frantic drive to get inside and to the boy who feels so close to death. Enraged, I shake him in disgust and throw him hard against the wall. He slumps, lifeless, into the rags. I realize, then, too late, that in my rage I've killed my only hope for help.

I fall onto my knees and wail.

the door speaks —

The man rises now and comes at me, enraged. He throws himself at me with such ferocity, I shudder with each blow. Not once, nor twice, but relentlessly, and recklessly he throws his frame against my wood; yet iron and stone and no small spell hold me fast against his vain attack.

I feel his shoulder crumple first. Yet, he comes at me again. I feel the breaking of his ribs. Spittle mixed with blood splatters cross my chest—his brawn and bone to no avail against the fortress of my Keep. Is it dumb fury or fool love or futile fantasy of chivalry—his flesh his sword, hell-bent to save an innocent-in-distress from tyrant, troll, or dragon-lord?

He's lost his mind, that's evident, but this is as it has to be; I open to no mean exercise of force. Nor does the knowledge he carries here from up above have any currency in this hall below. What he brings and trusts, a mere persona crafted long ago, when the child inside my door was banished here by pain so overwhelmingly severe his angels hoped to spare him grief. But they, in mercy then, made well what may become his grave.

Unless the man outside does what the Watcher of the Deep advised, the child who languishes inside my Keep will die.

It pains me to be a party to his ordeal. If I could help the man, I would. But the magic of the Earth, this alchemy, requires that I let him be.

Gods too long ignored have drawn, around the fortress-tower of his life, a storm. The rampart round his brain is crumbling with each blow, and now bereft of any strength he's known, he falls as if head-first into an abyss that runs far deeper than the pit to which he has already come.

the man speaks —

I'm fading now. It hurts me just to breathe. I've fallen down beside the door and slump against its frame—my bones no more capable of holding me erect than those of the broken wretch I threw against the wall. I pant for every breath, gasping at what little air will swell these now beleaguered lungs. I feel sick, as if I'll heave and empty myself of all I've tried to keep inside.

What stupidity ever to have veered from the path above and stepped into this Tree!

It comes. A great and frightful surge moves hard against the ragged shoreline of my life. Dark Grief rides the cresting wave, then slams down over me. It flattens me against the hard stone of the Earth. I cry. I sob. And try to catch my breath, caught in this paroxysm of unrelenting pain.

The surge has passed, but as it goes, I feel another rising in its place. It comes with such ferocity that what's left of life's knocked out of me.

Tears sting my eyes; they wet my cheeks. I gasp again for air. Too little comes. The flood's too thick, my strength too thin.

I'm drowning in this diluvium of despair.

the door speaks —

The man is fading. The vigor of his life pours out upon the floor. His eyelids flag—his flame is going out.

Suddenly I feel a tremor in my frame; the ancient hinges creak, the sands of time come hard against my wood, and like a flood, they make me open my old Keep.

A boy, balloon in hand, stands beside the fading figure of the man. In reverie, he gazes down upon his broken form; his eyes are bright, his face alight with innocence and joy.

The boy bends down to kiss his bloodied brow, then stoops to rest his head upon the withered breast of him so near to death. I watch, enthralled, as suddenly the boy falls down upon his chest, slips silently inside and disappears.

The man turns on his side, his eyelids flutter, he blinks, then opens wide his eyes. He coughs and heaves, as if he's just come up for air from the bottom of the sea. He gasps and pants for every breath. Propped up and on an elbow now, he surveys what he sees: the open Keep, the old man lying in a heap, dead beside the door.

He shakes his head as if in disbelief.

I watch him as he staggers to his feet. Once up, he draws another breath, this one deep and full of life. Steadied now, he begins to walk erect and tall—astonishing for one who was so near to death. He puts his foot upon the ancient stair, then turns for one last look toward me, the Keeper of the Deep. I see he's older now than when he first approached my door; his face is creased with age, the mantle of his hair now flecked with grey. His eyes—they are ablaze with light of an eternal day.

Then turning toward the hanging steps that brought him down into this place, he bounds up into the Pillar of the World, buoyed by a hundred thousand new-born stars shimmering gold against the dark of this abysmal space.

The song begins again. And he, united with the child that was lost, becomes a man at last, no more a shell of what a man can be.

a voice speaks—

Something familiar's hidden deep inside us all, beneath the trunk and canopy of these lives we know and see. Among our darkened roots there works a sacred alchemy.

As God once hid in one of humble birth, so too the thing of greatest worth conceals itself inside the basest stone. Gold is made when what we think we are, or hope to be, or proffer to the world so carefully, falls before the door of pain so bitter to our minds, we thought we'd locked it up for good and thrown away the key.

Those who waken from the trance produced by life upon the Plane, will face the truth that what we hate or hide or wish to disavow is what we can reclaim. These buried disowned parts of us possess a power that can make us whole.

Down in the dark is where we start the healing of the Earth, the rescue of our souls.